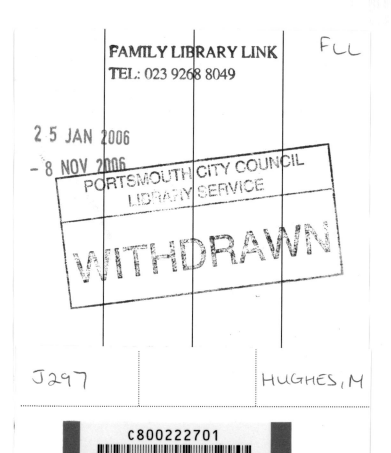

Festivals

My Id-ul-Fitr

Monica Hughes

Heinemann
LIBRARY

Little Nippers

www.heinemann.co.uk/library
Visit our website to find out more information about **Heinemann Library** books.

To order:
☎ Phone 44 (0) 1865 888066
🖷 Send a fax to 44 (0) 1865 314091
💻 Visit the Heinemann Bookshop at www.heinemann.co.uk/library to browse our catalogue and order online.

First published in Great Britain by Heinemann Library, Halley Court, Jordan Hill, Oxford OX2 8EJ, part of Harcourt Education. Heinemann is a registered trademark of Harcourt Education Ltd.

Editorial: Sarah Eason and Georga Godwin
Design: Jo Hinton-Malivoire and Tokay, Bicester, UK (www.tokay.co.uk)
Picture Research: Rosie Garai
Production: Séverine Ribierre

Originated by Dot Gradations Ltd
Printed and bound in China by South China Printing Company

ISBN 0 431 18633 2 (hardback)
07 06 05 04 03
10 9 8 7 6 5 4 3 2 1

ISBN 0 431 18639 1 (paperback)
07 06 05 04 03
10 9 8 7 6 5 4 3 2 1

British Library Cataloguing in Publication Data
Hughes, Monica
Little Nippers Festivals My Id-ul-Fitr
297.3'6
A full catalogue record for this book is available from the British Library.

Acknowledgements
The Publishers would like to thank Chris Schwarz and Trip/H. Rogers **p. 15** and Peter Sanders **p. 22** for permission to reproduce photographs.

Cover photograph of the children opening presents, reproduced with permission of Chris Schwarz.

The Publishers would like to thank the family and school involved and Philip Emmett for their assistance in the preparation of this book.

Every effort has been made to contact copyright holders of any material reproduced in this book. Any omissions will be rectified in subsequent printings if notice is given to the Publishers.

2

Contents

Id-ul-Fitr at school

We like making Id-ul-Fitr cards with our teacher.

Mum has her hands
decorated. Don't they
look beautiful?

Qur'an school

It's quite difficult to read the Qur'an in Arabic.

I know all my prayers very well.

Getting ready

I'm writing a card for
my cousins in Pakistan.

Mum makes special food for Id.
I like helping.

Mmm!

New clothes

My grandad sent me new
clothes as a present for Id.

Don't we look **smart!**

Ramadan ends

I like the dates we eat in the evenings of the month of Ramadan.

We say our prayers at home.

New Moon

We listen to the radio to hear if the new Moon has been seen.

15

Id night

I'm going to have some new bangles for Id.

17

The mosque at Id

Everyone goes to mosque at Id-ul-Fitr.

Presents at Id

It's nice to get presents,
but we remember to give money
to help other people too.

21

Family and friends

Yummy!

It's time for a delicious meal together.

What a **wonderful** Id party.

23

Index

The end

Notes for adults

Most festivals and celebrations share common elements that will be familiar to the young child, such as new clothes, special food, sending and receiving cards and presents, giving to charity, being with family and friends and a busy and exciting build-up time. It is important that the child has an opportunity to compare and contrast their own experiences with those of the children in the book. This will be helped by asking the child open-ended questions, using phrases like: What do you remember about …? What did we do …? Where did we go …? Who did we see …? How did you feel …?

Id-ul-Fitr is a Muslim festival that comes at the end of Ramadan, a month of fasting. The date changes so that Id-ul-Fitr is earlier each year, but lasts for three days after the new Moon appears. It is a time of thanksgiving with special prayers said at the mosque, lead by the imam. Families gather together and celebrate with other members of the community.

Follow up activities could include making an Id-ul-Fitr card for a Muslim friend using illustrations of flowers or decorative repeating patterns, tasting dates, making a cut-out hand shape and decorating it for Id-ul-Fitr and looking for examples of Arabic writing.

24